AF176364

**MIRRAN THOUGHT**

# MIRRAN THOUGHT
Spitzwiesenstr. 50
90765 Fürth
Germany

www.dwmirran.de
www.empty.de
empty@empty.de

# READ TWENTYFOUR
# (MT-629)

Print and Publication by BOD
In de Tarpen 42
D-22848 Norderstedt
www.bod.de
info@bod.de

First printing 2020

MIRRAN THOUGHT is the publishing arm of
Mirran Threat, a company devoted to releasing the
music and writings of the various members of Doc
Wör Mirran. Mirran Thought and Mirran Threat are
both divisions of MT Undertainment.

# Behold the
# Lovely Monster

# Joseph B. Raimond

Written in Nürnberg & Fürth, Germany
in the mid 1990s.

As always, in loving memory of Frank
Abendroth and Tom Murphy.

For Conny, my perfect angel.

Dedicated to John Lewis.

Cover art 2005, untitled,
by Joseph B. Raimond.

This is DWM release Nr. 179

## - AMBUSH -

I am fighting a battle
That I cannot win
The older I get
The harder it is to fight
Back

Tumors, fear of the untold
From the voice of medical authority
Or through my nourishment
I feel attacked from all sides
Ambush

I just want to whimper away
Dry up like a stinking puddle of piss
In the sun

Without pain
Without worry
To just evolve
Into

Nothing

## - BECKON ME AS HEAVEN -

The stars beckon me as heaven
And I yearn for their approval
As I reach up and try to grasp
Heaven
But all I feel is the dirty city air
Of hell

Your love beckons me as heaven
And I yearn for your approval
As I reach to you and try to grasp
Heaven
But all I feel are your problems
And my past life
In hell

## - REFUSING TO BE SPENT -

Currency notes
Declare denominations
By color
As racist

For the first time in history,
Lower denomination currency
Is on strike
Refusing to be spent
In what the more radical
Currency leaders describe
As a monetary
Civil war

## - DICKSEED -

Dickseeds flowing
Tubesteaks rising for the occasion
Shell to hell in a handbasket
Let their employees ride the waves of semen
As they jerk each other off with excuses
As to why we should buy the dickseed
Of their corporate elite fuckers
Who kill us for profit
And rape our mothers
I promised myself
That I will get revenge on these asswipes
And I never break a promise

## - KEEP ME BUSY -

I must write
To keep me busy
Salvation through the act of pretending
That what I write might be important
Someday

I must paint
To keep me busy
To plan on token exhibits of my work
All the while I like to think
That someone will want to
Write a book about me someday

I like to compose music
To keep me busy
Record it, release it
Sell a few dozen, and slowly go broke
While the worst shit ever
Shit upon the public
Sells millions and makes cretins rich

What the fuck
Is the point anymore
Of keeping me busy?

## - MY BELOVED KETCHUP-

My beloved ketchup
The bringer of scorn
The messenger of bad culture
Deliver unto me thy taste
Of preservatives
Forever preserving thy
Substandard tomatoes

Create for me from thy bottle
A burger able to conquer
My pangs of gluttony
Where the essence of fork and knife
Have no place of honour on thy table

My beloved ketchup
I will not forsake thee

## - FORGIVENESS-

I cannot forgive my body
For growing old
Without my consent

Permission withdrawn

My little boy will
And quest of play
Rages in this ol' bag o' bones
Sentenced to life?!?
What utter nonsense
My personal prison

I cannot forgive my bones
For creaking like
Grandma's old rocking chair

I cannot forgive my eyes
For blurring my vision of beauty

I cannot forgive my belly
For being the only part of my body
That is still growing

I cannot forgive my hair
At least those that I have left
For turning grey

I cannot forgive this body of mine
For accepting age in all its wrinkles
And will punish it accordingly

## - RED HAIR -

Red hair, glistens in the sun
The springtime has arrived, we have won
The iron clouds of waste though linger near
A lesson to, our conquered fear

Let the sunshine this teach you well
That always near, can linger hell
For the sake of our love, try block it out
Let our love be eternal, without a doubt

And be assured, in my heart to reside
Your red hair, forever not lied
Gather strength and love, don't we look back
For the sun stands before us
And hell at our backs

# - THE RELATIONSHIP OF HELL -

The fat beast
Stalking the earth
Killing its victims with loneliness
Black clouds of depression
To choke one's happiness

Total despair
It would wallow in self-hate
Drag everyone and everything
Down into
The relationship of hell

I should know
I was one of its victims
And I got the scars to prove it

## - MY SUN IS ALWAYS SETTING -

I've got that bad feeling
And it just doesn't go away anymore
My sun is always setting
And my dawn will never come

Attacked from all sides
I'm just a little boy at heart
I don't think I'll ever learn
To cope with this world
So why do I stay?

My sun is always setting
My days are growing colder
The days are growing shorter
And I'm starting to forget
How the good times were

I anticipate an endless night

## - WE ALL SUCK -

The days are gone
When people excite me
Or inspire me
To become anything other than
Average

Your parties bore me
Your music bores me
When the roll is taken
For the great achievers in art
Your name aint gonna be called
Dude

Maybe the problem
Is that we are all
Growing tired and old
Uninspired
And I see too much
Of your mediocrity
In myself
Face it, we all suck

I guess that is why
I am not popular anymore

## - MY BIG FAILURE -

It is always held against me
My failure to accept
What is gone, times gone past
My big failure

Too sentimental,
I have often been told
Longing for times that will never again be
I see the young just growing into their hormones
And it makes me long for that feeling again
The knowledge that I can do anything
That the world will revolve around me
That I will love and be loved
That I will be powerful and respected

Bus as the years roll by
Reality has bitten and bitten hard
For youth escapes through all our fingers
The difference between you and I
Is that I cannot accept it

## - RELIEF -

For the river
Relief is the lake of still water
After the waterfall

For the rain
Relief is the droplets of water
On the hood of the new car

For the wind
Relief is the plains of Oklahoma
Or the cornfields of my birth:
Nebraska

For me
Relief is the time between heartbeats
Flowing through my blood
Nourishment for my nerves

## - SCIENTIFIC THEORY -

Every increase on the
Technological meter
Creates an equal response
On the loneliness meter

The world is thrusting forward
Like some wild animal sex drive
Always better, faster, more
And I am being left behind
By the residue of change
And there are others out there like me
I see them by the hundreds
Dazed by unloving digital monitors
Rejected by gadgets too complicated to work

We are the sum
Of the scientific equation

## - MR. MUD -

Rush, rush, always in a rush
I walk parallel to the path
Better to walk among the soft blades of grass
Than stomp through the mud of the path
Today, I thought

The mud frowned and said:
"Can I help it if it rained last night?"

"The more you people walk along my edge,
In the grass,
The more the grass dies
And the wider I become
I want to stay thin, not become fat
I'm on a diet, so please walk on me"

I said I was sorry and stomped through his face
Later I had to clean up the little dried bits
Of his face
That had fallen off my shoes when I got home

Man, that's gratitude, huh?

## - MOMENTUM -

I would like to punch the guy
That invented momentum
For without this insidious
Contraption:

Car crashes would be harmless
All speed limits redundant
Your car's paint job would last forever
Gleaming without ever a dent

All handguns would become toys
And bullets could be used as firecrackers
War would be pointless
And we would not have to hold on tight
Before the subway started moving

Sex would not be much fun
And the makers of roller coasters
Would quickly go bust

First fights would be obsolete
For punches would not hurt

So that inventor guy better hurry
Before I find him

## - FOR BERNARD -

His quivering twitter quivered
And twittered until it
Could quiver no more
Then he died

## - LITTLE GREEN TITTIES -

Tiny jelly mounds
Chewy and minty tasting
Little green titties
To suck on

The little mini-nipples
Barely able to see with
The naked eye

I pop the
Little green titties
Into my mouth
Savour the minty taste
And think about you
And your big beige titties
And what they will taste like
Tonight

## - SUBSCRIPTION TO LIFE -

To whom it may concern:

Please do not renew my subscription
I can no longer afford the monthly payments
They are too expensive
It was not what I had been expecting
I can't make the deadlines
I have to give up too much
I am not ready for such a compromise
Your product did not live up to my expectations
It is simply no longer worth the cost

Sincerely,

Joseph B. Raimond

## - MY CUP OF HATE -

My cup of hate
Is overflowing with blood
Pooling in the dirt, ever growing
It is the juice of my depression
Of slit wrists and gunshot holes

Take a drink from my cup
And feel your happiness disappear
And your hope for a better world
Will bite the dust

Take a drink from my cup
And see your future for what it is
The grim reality of truth
My ultimate truth

My cup of hate
Serves reality

## - TEAR -

Silent night
The first fog that I greet tonight
Do you love me as I love you?
Will you stand at my side?
As I try to see it through

You peep through the lamppost's light
As if in a smile, I swear
I shiver in the December night
For the cold rips at my skin, tear

The blackness of this night of all
For the millions try to forget you
They crash their cars
And hang themselves by the neck
For they can't face what you are
What you do

Tonight is the night
That the loneliness comes down to bear
Their waves of alcohol and entertainment
Will not protect them this time
For the cold rips at their selves, tear

## - FRINGES -

Truthful expression is worthless today
Nobody cares if your heart bleeds truth
Nobody cares if you stand naked in expression
You will die from the frost
Of their cold indifference

For they are too busy
With their mass-produced stars
Technological falsehood to hide
The quick buck
You and I, the real artists
Are destined to die on the fringes
Our paintings unseen, our books unread
And nature, the mother of our inspiration
Is being killed by the waste of public
Consumption, greed
When she has died
Too, shall I be dead

## - DOWN UNDER -

Down under, depths
Nothing to lose
Because one can only go up from here
The stink of alcohol is the proof
Of a quick attempt at forgetting a problem
A problem that is destined
To rule my world forever

Where you should help me to rise
To shine
You keep pushing my head under

Where you should be there for me
When I just can't go on anymore
You are nowhere to be found

You magnify my ugly past
Until it surrounds me, envelopes me
A life of its own, devouring me

I now live in the bowels
Of your jealousy monster
Down under, in the stink of hate
Slowly being digested

You say there is nothing left to save
How right you are
For who would want what comes out
Of a monster's bowels?

## - BAY AREA POEM -

A block above the sky
Where the waters mix and embrace
The barking seals accompany our thoughts
As we embraced and undressed
Making love while being loved
By the California sun as it shown
Into our hearts and capturing us
Forever,
Filling us with a hunger
A longing of what could be
Anticipation
Of what might be
You now own us,
We belong to you
Forever

## - LOVE OF FREE RAIN -

Emotion dictates
Actions without purpose
Frozen rain
Forever rationalizing you
You,
You,
Distant you

Heart pounding over
Friendly gestures
Never knowing
The love of free rain

## - SYNTAX VS. INCOME TAX -

If only I had never been born
I would not have had to have paid
Income tax
For income tax is a
Prerequisite for life
For to have had to have lived
One must have had to have accepted death
And tax
To have had to have paid tax
Is to have lived having to pay taxes
And have had to have accepted it

Life is to have had been born
And the taxman will have calculated
How much income tax
You will have had to have paid in your life
Only then will you have had the permission
To die

## - I DON'T KISS ASS FOR A LIVING -

Huh? What was that?
You serious?
Sorry, unlike some people I know
I don't kiss ass for a living

Hard work, sweat
A little inspiration
And mostly tears
And I might scrape by

Still, with all your money and possessions
You look up to me, as if to belittle
Your own gift of politics
Something which I honestly want
But only when I'm feeling uninspired

If I only possessed the power
Of politics
I could triumph, win any race
But maybe I should be happy
With my power for compassion
And love for creation
Which just might be my ticket
To immortality

## - YOUR PROBLEM -

When I hold your hand
I feel your problem

When we kiss
I taste your problem

When we talk
We talk about your problem

When we make love
I make love to your problem, not to you

When I look into your eyes
I see not love for me
But your love for your problem
And I become jealous

## - SLEEPING SUCCESSFUL -

Sleeping successful
The day awake
Produces only repetition
Experiments reveal the happy surprise

Longing for the falling leaves
Pointing the way to accidental success
In the beauty of the white, unassuming world
In memories as you gaze out
Of the ugly window

Take leave
Temporary wisdom
Never revealing
Your frivolous speech

Make way, make way
Time promises a return to the fog
Days under the sun
And sleeping successful

## - CHANGE (THE POEM) -

Once upon a time
I fought you, hated you
Like everyone does
For you took from me what I loved
The things I considered mine

But now I know
That I must not fight against you
But embrace you, love you
For to work with you,
And encourage you
Is to possess infinite strength
Strength that my enemies,
Can never understand, nor equal

Change brings life
Change brings death
And death is better than no change
For no change is nothing

## - TOTAL DESPAIR -

Total despair
Is the noose
Around my neck

Total despair
Are the wheels
As I'm cut in half

Total despair
Are little white pills
As I fall asleep

Total despair
Is red blood
As it comes from my arm

Total despair
Is the blade
Pierced my heart

Total despair
Is the earth
Coming to me

Total despair
Is pure hate
Is pure hate

Nothing to say

I've found the way
Leave this place
And the human race

Yes it's sick
Done the trick
It's coming on
I'll soon be gone

## - BEHOLD THE LOVELY MONSTER -

Behold the lovely monster
Her wayward teeth, short lived and brown
Like kicking the corpse of the maggot
Who was destined always to be ugly

Death and the judge
Presiding over the court of the hideous
They are prepared to sentence the accused
To a life of life

Behold the lovely monster
Obnoxious, the clouds of depression
Like a fog of blue, descends on the accused
And treats him to a healthy taster, dose
Of what awaits him as he pays his debts
To a sick society, his own
Free of charge of course, and tax deductible

His only friend, the yellow rubber-duckie
Scowls, has now grown the teeth of hunger
And hate
As he bathes, scrub
Trying to wash off the filth of guilt
The chomp comes, delivers the promised
Pain
As the penis of the accused
Is severed

But no blood is delivered from the wound
As he must live to carry out his sentence
The puzzle though is complete,
And he has lost the game of death
Behold the winner
Behold the lovely monster

## - YOU ONCE -

You once game me joy
Now I feel only sadness

You once gave me understanding
Now you give me accusations

You once made me feel loved
Now you say you hate me

You once gave me the feeling that I could
Conquer the world
Now I have trouble facing each day

You once made me want to scream to the world
That I love you
Now you tell me not to bother saying it anymore

You once gave me a reason to live
Now I am not so sure I want to anymore

## - THE OLD LADY BRIGADE -

At any given time
In any German city
Take a look up at the windows
And you will always see
A member of Germany's elite force

You hear so much talk
Of the ex-DDR Stasi
But the real evil is still with us
Re-united Germany's millions
Of meddling old ladies

For not a window be broken
Nor a car double parked
Will escape the wrath
Of this elite fighting force

## - ROUTINE OF PAINS -

There it is again
That pain in my chest
Shortness of breath
I feel like an old man
Is it finally the big one?

Day after day
Same old thing
Routine of pains
Routine of boredom, uninspired
The only thing keeping me awake
Are the pains in my chest
The only thing keeping me painting
Is the fear of death

## - ICE-AGE -

Boiling hot
So fuckin' hot
The sun, shining on my skin
Cooking, burns by skin

But my heart stays cold
The ice-age of my soul
So frozen, no sun can wake
Nor the threat of hell can thaw
Nor the love of my woman can crush
Laying as a monster in hate, ready

## - THE ROBOT NEEDS NO LIGHT -

I want to feel again
Help me get back to sunshine
Working all night
The robot needs no light

Build for his divine purpose
He functions without emotion
Obeying the commands
That will someday destroy him

## - WHERE DID I LEAVE MY HEAD? -

Stress
I am running around in circles
My mind is off in another corner of the world
Trying to sort out some problem
While my body attempts to perform
Basic physical tasks
Nothing is working, there is no coordination
Did I leave the coffee machine turned on?
Will my apartment burn down?
Where did I leave my head?
What is your name?
Hurry, the dog needs to be walked
Stress
Stress
Shit, I missed the bus
Don't forget to have the kid brush her teeth
Did she get her homework done?
What about the changes to the contract?
Is that sentence in the future tense
Or should it be passive?
Did I pay that bill to the lawyer?
Stress
I think I left the basement light burning
What is the difference between
Dative and accusative?
I am running around in circles
Did she remember to stub out her cigarette?
Stress
My mind is off in another corner of the world

Suing you in a court of law
What time does the train leave for Erlangen?
What is your name?
When is their next live show?
Stress
Stress…..

## - OLYMPICS -

I'm so tired of playing
This game of hate with you
A sport where I always lose
Because I don't like the rules

## - I'M RESPONSIBLE-

I'm responsible:
For making you cry
For our arguments
For your general unhappiness
For your depression
For the depressions of all those around me
For the mental disorders of the lazy pig
For Peter's car not starting this morning
For alienating our friends from us
For the high crime rate in our fair city
For your favorite party not getting elected
For our polluted river
For all natural catastrophes
For teen suicide
For world hunger
For coronary heart disorders
For nuclear annihilation
For death

# - MRS. FATSO HAS NOTHING TO EAT -

Mrs. Fatso has nothing to eat
She's got lots of clothes
But nothing to eat
She spends her days
Pulling bricks from the streets

Mrs. Fatso is real

## - I'M NOT ALLOWED -

To eat cooked vegetables
To wash the dishes
To relax after work
To leave the house without combing my hair
To have a more stressful job
To listen to my music
To paint without explanations
To lead a normal life
To learn from my mistakes
To love my woman
To look towards the future
To forget my past
To just be me

## - UNINSPIRED-

Sometimes I feel so uninspired
Numb to the bone, ice clogged blood
Where no one, not even fat women
In stretch pants
Can inspire an ugly painting

Uninspired to the point of no return
Where children's laughter bounces
Off the old man's wrinkled cheeks
Not even a glimmer of nostalgia
Reaches the deaf ears

Uninspired to the point of machinery
Where gears and programs dictate
The art that is on today's agenda

Uninspired to the point of death
Where even the fear of death
Does not indulge one to the point of a poem
For ice in the heart is already
Like being dead

## - EVERYBODY -

Why does everybody
Have their own face
But still
All the look the same?

And they all have feelings
And want to be loved
And they are all so lonely
Like me

I don't like the smell of sex

# - STUPID PEOPLE, SMART PEOPLE -

Stupid people drive cars
Smart people ride the subway

Stupid people
Honk at each other for pausing too long
At the stop sign

Smart people
Yell at each other for blocking
The subway doors

Stupid people
Smash into each other's cars
And pay a lot for insurance

Smart people
Pay 50 Deutschmarks for a month-pass
And hope the signals
Work properly

## - I WILL FIGHT! -

I will fight
For my right to:

Cause myself pain
Stick needle-nose plyers up my nose
Make myself miserable
Battery acid enemas on the house!
Be down in the dumps
Both literally and figuratively
Eat shit, let myself be bought out
Resold and marketed
Snorting, sporting and supporting
A brown nose

Yes, I will fight!

## - A BLIND HIPPY -

Almost every time I saw
A blind hippy to send me money,
Honey
And I can't even see

I am a nightmare
Filled to the rim
With paranoia
Of seeing perfect lips

## - I GUESS-

No matter how bad things get
How hungry the heart becomes
I guess
I should always be grateful
That I will never:

Like the taste of liver
Smoke
Become a junkie
Become a sports fan
Join a bowling league
Own a Mercedes
Enjoy my job
Live in New Jersey
Work as a steward on a Boeing 747
Paint like Norman Rockwell
Draw like Albrecht Dürer
Play guitar like Eddie Van Halen
Sign to a major record label
Buy Richard Marx albums
Fuck Madonna
Go to a Rollins Band concert
Kiss ass for a living
Kill another human being
Meet everyone who buys my books
Live forever

## - FRAU CITY -

Hustle bustle
Frau city
You don't appeal to me
Anymore
Your exhaust fumes
Are worse
That a case of
Bad B.O.

You're getting fat in your
Suburbs
And your heart has a case
Of urban decay

I want a divorce

I want to marry
Mother nature
She may be a little sick
But she always looks
Young

## - NOTHING LEFT TO SAVE -

Cold wind blows
Through my hair,
Through my heart
Both are damp & worthless
Dirty

But it doesn't matter
Because there is nothing left to save
Hearts, love can only take so much
Of the weight of guilt
Before they break with sorrow
Or indifference
And then there is nothing left to save

For like death
And a form of death it is
There is no turning back
Or turning one's back to the death
Of life and love,
Happiness and peace
When there is nothing left to save

It does not matter anymore
There will come no more tears
From these eyes

## - PARANOID -

Are you really paranoid
Over the fat beast
With rings of obesity
With the foul smell of laziness
With her stench of stupidity
Quite simply
The uglies thing
Ever to walk this earth

Night and day
Black and white
It's so easy for me to see
And I know in my heart
How much you mean to me
So you see
Paranoid is the last thing in the world
You need to be

## - CLUMPS OF SHIT -

Scratch this
Cross out that
It is a wonder I get anything
Written at all

Where is the flow?
Why does it only come in
Clumps?
The most of which
Are clumps of shit

I must have this flow
Beautiful words, dark associations
The velocity of my philosophy
I want to conquer the world
With my pen

## - TRUCKER SLUT -

Eat me
Then go to hell
I don't want to see your bouncing titties
Ever again
Wipe that cheap red lipstick
Off my cock before I
Smash your worthless skull in
Don't even look at my Peterbuilt
I might let you ball me again
If I ever roll into Dayton, sometime soon
Hell, you should be paying ME, for doing you
So damn good
You could be Dolly Parton's little sister
I did her once too coming out of Nashville
I wrote her number here in my little black book
Aint that Loretta on the radio?
Turn it up, you
Ten four, good buddy!

## - <u>NOR EVEN CARE</u> -

Insecure
It has all been done before
(but not by me)

Tired of the work
Tired of the silence
Messages blurring, fading
It doesn't even matter
That no one sees it

I can no longer write, paint or talk
Nor even care

## - INDECISIVENESS -

Get out of town
Indecisiveness
Each and every step
Must be planned

Otherwise,

One walks
But gets nowhere

One breathes
But does not live

One sees
But does not understand

One listens
But does not hear music

One eats
But does not taste

One likes
But does not love

## - STUTTERS WITH RAGE -

The workaholic engine inside
Stutters with rage
As it loses its power
And to think I always thought
I needed more power

Maybe what you represent to me
Is more important than who you are

## - I DON'T KNOW -

I don't know
I don't know
I don't know

I don't know
Where I want to be
I just know
That I don't want to be here

I don't know
What I want to do
I just know
That I don't want
To do this anymore

I don't know
Where I have been
I don't know
Where I am going
I don't know
How to love
I don't know
How to accept love
I don't know
Who I am

I don't know
I don't know
I don't know

## - I AM WHAT I AM -

Let me dig
Moles need neither eyesight
Nor a blue sky

Let me tunnel beneath your feet
For I am the lowest of the low
Your lowest priority
Less than nothing
Not worth your love nor affection
Not worth your spittle
Or even a kind thought

Dogshit reeks on the surface
Smelly, rotten, sour with flies
I am lower, for I tunnel beneath it
My place is among dirt

## - NAME, RANK AND SERIAL NUMBER -

The horror
Of the yellow brick road, is that
It was all a film, nothing more
The reality of the monster in your heart
Is what scares me most

Mountains of mole-hills, the reach for sky
By grubby little hands, the ilk of which
Feed your ugly egos

A battalion of egos, from which
You will stand victorious
Our puny little onslaughts of wit
You can conquer with one foul look and a word
On the side

I stand defeated, on the battlefield of
What was once probably love
But is now indifference, no man's land
I will lick my wounds and become a
Prisoner of war
Sorry, name, rank and serial numbers only
You can interrogate me on my motives
I will stand occupied, a spoil of war, silent
As I rot in my cell, I look out for hours into
The fields of love, blossoming
And see moles reaching for the sky
But no yellow brick road

## - RESIDE -

I'm not alive

Oh, sure
I eat, shit and urinate
I sleep, breath and
Bleed when cut

I walk, talk and have an opinion
I can think, respond and
Kick your ass if you piss me off

But my soul is gone
A void of nothingness
Less that the nothing between the stars
Has inherited the space
Where my love once resided
Gone on a permanent vacation
Of endless summer days,
Getting laid and drinking beer
Back to the time of a promise filled youth
Unaccepting of change and age
Gone, to wait out the day
Of my inevitable, physical deadness

## - ABSURD -

Run around aimless
Watch out, don't be late
Frenzy of absurdity
And purple bumps on my head

The appointment rules my life
My sign is the chicken
With its head cut off
Forever embroidered in the lazy stars
For all to see
And astrolize

## - ROCK MUSIC -

Your rock music is dull
Boring beats, the bass is a drag
The guitar just goes
Twang, twang, twang
Like a typical drizzly, dark
German day

Boring as fuck!

Who needs it?
Who buys it?

Not me!

## - OCEAN STORM -

Salty water
And the sun is going down
A grey mountain
Off in the                distance
Oh, yes
The one hill in this land
Of salt
Of the prankster

## - NUMB -

I have lost all ability to feel

When the rain cries
I no longer taste its despair
When the sun shines,
The shadow of my indifference
Blocks the love in its rays

I sit and plan each day
Every minute
Of every day is planned and accounted for
In minute detail
And there is no more time left
For feeling

## - <u>YOU'RE A SNAKE</u> -

You're a snake
Slither and slime
Politics at heart
Soulless and cold
Even your own family
Thinks you're a creep

I'm not useful enough
You used me, abused me
So politics of friendship
I had given you

Distrust has destroyed
No, you are not my friend
Earned so much hatred
Will you learn in the end?

So slither and slime
Yourself to your grave
Cold blooded, alone
Too late to be saved

## - THIRTY THREE -

A critical stage
From which no music emanates
At age 33
I have now finally been confronted with
Some fuckin' depressin' realities

That I will never:

Drive a streetcar
Fly in space
Become a vampire
Meet John Lennon
Make love to Kate Bush
Be a porno star
Go back to college
Learn to like Dali
Become a millionaire
Become immortal
Record in Abbey Road Studios
Sell stocks on Wall Street
Fuck Madonna
Live in Paris
Be a convicted serial killer
Be a rock and roll star
Release records on Sub Pop
Appreciate opera
Bring Zappa back from the dead
Learn to be happy

## - COAL IN MY EYES -

I see coal in my eyes
There are red lights all
Around me
And yet mother and I
Are walking
Although it is
Almost nine
I must go
I must go
The record stopped
My heart stopped
And I can't stop
Writing
Writing

God
My shower is leaking
It sounds like the
Birds back home
God I loved that voice
That brought us all together
It forever whispers
In our soul
The voice is dying
But it is still there
Though always getting
Smaller
Smaller
Like the bus to school

And back
And back

## - MY WRITTEN WORD -

My written word
Has only been conceived
For my pleasure maybe
Or to define my brief life

My written word
Tries to make sense
Out of the jumble of my thoughts
Easing my confusion, into art

My written word
Does not exist to please you
A forlorn public with your own
Definition of fame
Different from my own

My written world
Exists as if my child
And I will die to protect it
As ferocious as a mother bear
In a rage

My written word
As my offspring
Is destined to outlive me

My written word
Is sometimes born premature
Death, still on my mind

As a forgotten thought
Before it is born unto paper
And given life immortal

## - GONNA LIMIT MYSELF -

Gonna limit myself
To a slow death

Step 1: Where I can no longer smell fresh air

Step 2: I cannot see the orange sunset

Step 3: I don't enjoy walking in the rain

Step 4: my lover is no longer my friend

Step 5: my heart stops from numbness

Death,
I'm almost there

## - BILL -

Bill, the man
I will take the truth in your colours
Alcohol stained or not, spelling
The choice is yours

Over the certificate of show
Parody of what you already know
With their iron suits of ego
The certainty of success echoes in their eyes
But you and I know better
Disgruntled or not
Bitter or not
Does not change the fact
That those state certified
"Artists"
Will be selling us pencils within 5 years

## - AUTOMATIC -

The days are just automatic
The assembly line life
Numb is the name of the game
And the rules are dictated by
Cold

The days are just automatic
They slip away so quickly
One by one, dripping my life away
Into the pool of indifference and
Middle age

I'm losing my love of life
Each day past is yet another day
Away from my youth and towards
An ultimate numbness

Like grasping for straws
I am desperate to hold onto my youth
My memories of good times
And the warmth of my friends

## - PONDER-

Squeaking, honk
The rusty playground, joints in need of oil
Behind my back, the children play
As the sun is setting
They must soon go to bed

Behind my back, the world is plotting
To seal my money by official means
As they wait for my death,
Marriage

I sit on a park bench at night
Ponder my loneliness
As I often do
And think about squeaking and honking
Who is responsible for playground
Maintenance
And bedtime stories untold

## - RESTLESS-

I'm being torn apart
Thousands of little lonely pieces
Each with a longing of its own
To explore and love each nook and cranny
Before turning to dust, worthless

Restless, I feel longing
For places I've never known
But which call on my heart
An unyielding, barrage
Of unwelcome magnetism
I'm waging a war
That no one else can feel
And there are no winners
Just one big loser:
Me

## - FAME-

Jah live
But I am not allowed of it
The taste of such fruit
Is foreign to me tongue
For I and I are not permitted
To be a connoisseur to my art
The tastes of my fruit
Lie tasteless and bland to you
Uncooked, raw
Never to be served in my lifetime

## - PARADOX-

I am this paradox
In flesh and in soul
I am equally the victim of the crime
And the hero of the war

You say my eyes, so blue
Shine with understanding
But I feel the death lurking
Behind, and the tears that want to swell

You feel my body as it loves you
Yields to you, your demands, and becomes yours
Yet I fell the sickness in my veins
The quiet yet steady processes
That only can lead to the numb

You say that I look so young
Surprised at the truth of my years
Yet my mind is that of an ancient man
Tired, in need of rest
Subtle coma that no interest can cure

I am the paradox
In flesh and in soul
I am equally the victim of my crimes
And the hero of my war

## - FOR MY PAL BERND-

Going to fly through the land of cotton
And feel weightless for awhile
Guided by my will for change
Finally a bit of anticipation, for once
For something good
That might lie ahead

Out of that dreary basement hole
Six years of stale air
Bad lighting, and worse music
Have given me the edge
For the lust for life

So I am off!
Dream come true!
Gonna quack like the platypuses.
Gonna howl with the dingoes,
Gonna hop with the kangaroos,
Oh, hop with joy!

# - ANTS, LIKE THE SPECKS THEY ARE-

Millions, billions,
(Soon to be) trillions
The ugly masses
Turning in, flipping out
Pretending each and everyone
Is important

With their petty little worries
And their petty little love affairs
With their petty little births
And their even less important
Deaths

Enough is enough
Step on them with random abandon
Squash, meaningless
Ants, like the specks they are

Insects and humans
Bugs and people
Same species
Different colored eyes

## - MY SUN IS ALWAYS SETTING (REMIX)-

Got that bad feeling
Don't go away no more
My sun is always setting
Dawn will never come

Attacked from all sides
Just a little boy
Don't think I'll ever learn
To cope with this world

My sun is always setting
Days are growing shorter
Days are growing colder
The day is about to die

The endless night is coming
The night it wants to kill me
The night it wants my blood
The night has killed my sun

My sun is always setting
My sun is always setting…

## - MY VERSION OF THE MORNING-

Loud, distorted
Garbled voices pound my sweet dream
Forever into forgetfulness, never to be returned
As I want to pound those lousy transistors
A cheap scapegoat for my own failure
To rise above the nine to fivers, scorned

I drag this old bag of bones
Into the wash closet to wash, piss
Away the remnants of cheap beer
The cold tiles of the bathroom floor,
Another object of my anger
Causing me to shiver and piss
All over the toilet seat

Stomach is a cramp, all it craves is coffee
Gulp down the boiling liquid,
As I tie my punk rock combat books, remnant
High ideals for a shallow shell, gone

Brush my yellowing teeth, not because of
Prevention
But out of habit
Sour breath to boot, curls the nose hairs

I look into the eyes of that thing in the mirror
I see the beginnings of gray and wrinkles
Encroaching death and despair
A tear as a sacrifice to lost ideals

Glistens in the light of the bare bathroom bulb

But got to hurry, catch the bus,
Hop the train
Can't be late to be at the place I hate!

Strain to find a seat and stare at all the ugly
Faces
I hate them and I know they hate me
For we all recognize the face of failure
We all wear the same mask

## - GRANTED-

I take everything for granted
The smell of a fresh rain
My cold feet after a snowstorm
The sun on my face
The laughter of my children
The smell of freshly cut grass
The smell of frying bacon
The sound of a David Gilmour guitar solo
The love of my mate
The love of my daughter

It is only when I am old
And on my deathbed
Good for nothing but as worm food
That I will see the mistake I have made

I will bug the nurse for friendship
And she will rightfully ignore me
And laugh about my folly to her co-workers
In their break room
As they smoke their cigarettes
She will tell of the crazy old man
Who wants to go outside in the rain

She will let me die
And not learn from my mistake

## - MURDERER-

I sit here, stumped
The blank page is my friend
Ally against those that try to defeat me
For his plainness is his virtue
He can end up, either as a poem
A drawing or a painting
He can draw you to despair
Make you cry with rage or joy
Bore you or adore you
Inspire you

Or kill you

## - PROUD -

Gonna practice some self-editation here
A little personal censorship
Can go a long way to quell
The mother's distaste
Of her son's affliction

Besides
It aint that hard
To keep
Yo mamma proud

## - LITTLE LOVERS SAY -

Little lovers say
They would die for you
Little lovers feel
That their love
Can conquer the world

Let's get real here
Insignificance!
So fuckin' little
Compared to
What is out there

So why bother?

## - OF ME -

Someday soon
I think
You will see
That I can't deliver
What you expect
Of me

I'm so
Set on my mission
It's hard
To give you any
Of me

And even
If there was anything
Left
I'm not sure
I
Would recognize it

## - THE ARTILLERIZATION -

For god's sake,
Hold your tongue and let me work
Wishful thinking of vacuumed floors
Walked dogs, errands to be run
Less than last priority, so get lost
Take a hike and stop feeling sorry for
Yourself

My own choice, like a river set free
Finds its own course and
Makes its own banks of compromise

Stop trying to rule me
And let me get back to work

# - PETRARCH NEVER GOT LAID -

Come down from the perch of souls
To a land of reality, material
See what is around you
And begin grabbing
While the grabbing is good

Surely there must be the odd
Literature groupie
Waiting for you in the back room
Of the library

For all I care, let you soul
Swish around up there, ethereal
Let it keep all your overblown
Philosophies company
But meanwhile, don't forget your hands
When learned properly,
Can feel you to
Ecstasy

Parallel with your soul
Yet anchored to reality

And helping to defy certain
Death

## - UNTITLED FOR OBVIOUS REASONS -

So fuckin' average
In everything
So why bother?

Maybe a changing of the ways
Is in order

Become a mass murderer
Surely that can't be very hard
Sure to get attention

Or maybe a serial killer
Get all those conjugal visits in prison
By death groupies with spread legs
And fan mail from deranged punk bands

Or just a plain old thug
Ruthless and cruel
Without inhibitions or scruples
Ugly personality and a chip on the shoulder

Yep

## - YOUTH -

Little boys of lust
Twelve years old and already
A jerk-off expert
Still searching in vain
For that first pubic hair

Little girls of lust
Eleven years old
And already sprouting boobs
Proud of their first bras
And still thinking of boys
As a little icky

## - <u>SCATTERBRAIN</u>-

Help me get my thoughts together
Everything's, uh, fragmented, getting
My vision is fading
To being forgotten
My vision of total control
Of my world and of my art
To conquer the world

It's been so many years
Since I've felt anything
I can hide permanent
Behind my numbers

## - PUPPET OF A TYRANT -

Control
Control
It's all about control
The strings may be invisible
But they are still
As strong as chains

## - BASEBALL SHADOW -

I'm afraid of the baseball shadow
Your machines may find hiding
Sucking
My war towards the impossible
Unhealthy, then dead
Not destined for a legend
Fit maybe for a tear or two
But no more

Don't rob me, it's not fair!

# - RACEHORSE -

Stress, run, quick
Don't miss that bus
Eat on the run, my stomach hurts
Gotta piss like a racehorse
Quick, paint a few dabs of color
On my masterpiece
While she's in the shower
Maybe she won't notice

I'll let that music inspire my soul
But only if I've got a few minutes to spare

I'll stop for just a minute
Think about how I once loved her
And then the phone will ring

## - BRAINWASH -

Flipper stayed at my house once
Um…
Flipper stayed at my house once
Um, well…
Flipper stayed at my house once
It's like…
Flipper stayed at my house once
Um, you know…
Flipper stayed at my house once
Cool man, like…
Flipper stayed at my house once
It's sort of, you know…
Flipper stayed at my house once
Hey, it's like…
Flipper stayed at my house once
Um…
Flipper stayed at my house once
Like…
Flipper stayed at my house once
You know what I'm sayin'…
Flipper stayed at my house once
It's cool, like, um…
Flipper stayed at my house once

Forget it,
You wouldn't understand anyway

## - KRITIQUE -

Doctor professor, stuffy so-and-so
Impresses in all that he learned and knows
His office displays this proof,
And it graces the walls

As we knock, we are allowed in
From the stuffy, smoke-filled halls

We are told not to be late,
But to listen, obey and learn
And if we pass
In the end,
We receive the award
That for which we have earned

But like troopers
It is not preferred
To step out of line
For to question the gods
Is like that of a sin
For which we will be punished
And fined

We all pretend to be of science
With formulas, footnotes
And our favourite theories
For an art that must breathe
Life to live
And from science grows weary

We are given the brush,
Colour and canvas
But told not to paint
For our own efforts to be deemed
Unworthy
Bad grammar, and quaint

When the hours are late
And the homework all done
I sit in my humble chamber,
And ponder the gone
The writers we aspire
To
The greatest of the age
How they would laugh
At our interpretations
Of their fun
And nonsenses on the page
At pulling our legs

So, I receive my pen
And begin to write
Of all this is wrong
In the world
And yes, the bit
That also seems right
Of my emotions, my dreams
And of my hate
Of inspiration and of love for a mate

And my words are pure,
They are as pure as me
For they and I are one
Eternally
And they are worth more to me
Than you
Can ever know
As you study only the past
Pretend to science
And grow old

## - BORDEAUX MASK -

The face of anger
Paranoid anxiety
I am wearing
The Bordeaux mask

How much time will it take
How often must I grind my teeth
How many sleepless nights
Must I withstand
How many vengeful daydreams
Will I still
Ponder
?
Before I learn
How to brush it aside
Harden my shell
And
Take off
My Bordeaux mask

## - J. SELVIN -

Joel Selvin can't dance
He picks his nose
And fries abortions for lunch
While waving at the pretty girls with his little
Hard-on

You lively old fart!

He twirls around, ridiculous
Spinning singles in one hand
And trying to cover his bald spot,
Glistening in the neon classroom lighting,
With the other

## - JOINTS -

Concentration problems
What was I.......?!?
Damn!

The only constants, aggravating
Piles of unfinished poems
A constant state of non-inspiration
And age, straining and paining
My joints

## - TOUCH WITH MY BREATH -

Your wicked tongue
Draws the time of breaking
Ever closer

So near, touch with my breath
The darkness of that fact

The nasty words, unthought
Yet uttered, but
Slice and wound, so near
To my heart
And so far from yours

# - METAPHOR -

Like a car with square wheels
A post office without stamps
A supermarket with no TV-dinners
A train with no tracks

Like a washing machine,
With no water hook-up

Like a magazine with no pages
Like a book with no words
Like a record with no sound
Like a movie with no actors
Or a porno-star with no penis

Like a vegetarian crocodile
Or giraffe allergic to leaves

Like a fish that can't swim
Or a bird with a fear of heights

I am human
But with no heart

## - THE RED WHEELBARROW -

(a new version for modern times)

So much depends
Upon

A red blood
Splatter

Mixing with rain
Water

Beside the black
Victim

## - B. WEBER -

One eyed blind
Yet intelligence's domain in the dark
Accidents were never a hinderance
And the sun was still a friend

The other eye
Defect, almost black and white
Yet learned to the degree of a master
It works too perfect for its own abilities
For pictures more real and living
Than mechanicals
Photos

And the jokes, my god!
From under which rock
Were they dug out from?
Birthed from the only genius
To ever build a radio-controlled shark
To scare and to teach
The boring old men's club
A lessen they will never forget,
Yet earned
In spades
Revenge for the ingenious,
And splinters galore!

A mansion full of
Parts and pieces,
To build and invent

Rend and repair
Millions of good ideas,
Enough for more than one lifetime

I saw the portrait you painted
Of your friend
Jacque Cousteau
As real as a photo
Standing in defiance
On the bottom of the sea
Later stolen,
While you were going into the ground
By your disgruntled
Long lost son

Or your portrait
Of your friend
Jack Kerouac
Naked as a beatnik should be
Pink Cadillac and all
Golden gate in the background
Small, but beautiful
And hanging proudly
Thousands and thousands
Of miles away
In my humble house

It has been decided upon, to depart
Which in reality is really worth a tear

Or two,
But that is a secret
For tears never fit into this picture

So long to your shark
Your paintings
Your piles of dusty
Bits and pieces
Of electronic junk
Your bad jokes

So long
To your terribly annoying
Bagpipes

San Francisco
Will never be the same

So long, Bill

## - TITAN -

Huge and
Rumble, luxury crumble
Awe inspired
To love

Fire and ice, love and hate
Burn and freeze intense
Parallel, if only for a few
Blinks of a beautiful eye

Shortly, it is over
The actors and actresses depart
For home, to husbands, wives, kids
Secret affairs
To family pooch
Routine

It is their job
To give us a reality
That is not real
Reel

They did their jobs well
Perhaps too well
For I have a rumble
In my heart
For an intense love
For an intense life
For an intense death

Life,
But of hours
Love enough
For an eternity

.

## - PRECARIOUS -

Everything is so precarious
A subtle change can evolve itself
Into a life or death situation
Security of possessions, or not
The luxury of love and sex,
Or not
And a new birth

## - CLOUDS -

Flying through the clouds
In a state of death
Becoming one with form
Color and music
Freedom, pure
Becoming everything
And yet nothing
Being everywhere
And yet still
Nowhere

## - GROUNDPOUNDER -

A pound
For some Ezra Pound
On the bus

Loveliest liveth your ghost in the crowd
Gas pedals in a dirty, stinking world

## - BILLBOARDS -

They're here
They're there
They are fuckin' everywhere
(except in Pine Valley and Santa Cruz)

Pound, pound, pound,
Worse that the childhood bully
They beat you
Into a consummating pulp

And the cost!
They are more fuckin' expensive
Than you can imagine!
I should know, man!
I checked!

Considering how many
Fuckin' people
Inhabit this poor, ailing
Planet
It is unbelievable
How little of our humanity
Once can experience
On the billboards
On our streets

I choose not to purchase

## - SUCKS -

Reality sucks,
And it's been sucking pretty bad lately

Souring relationships
Could use an extra star or two
During the midnight trek through
Difficult times, to give a bit of hopefulness
And maybe just a little more light

Too much work
(and we all know that work sucks bad)
To confuse my mission
Which way to turn and
How many percentage points does he get?

Body parts falling apart
Getting winded by a little wind
Gut pains and missed buses
Gotta lug all those extra tires everywhere
I go!

Failing memory and confusion
What was I writing about?
Arguments about nothing makes
Nothing so important
Fucking sucks
Sucks
Sucks
Sucks

Banish sucks,
And everything might just be OK

## - ASSUME -

Pissed off and drunk
3 a.m. on a country road
On the way home
From the worst concert
That ever was played

Something to burn
Was not even something to watch

Suddenly,
A loud thump
The car is brought to a stop
"What was that?" asks the
Vegetarian

"Probably a fox
And it must be dead, so keep
On driving"
Remarks the meatitarian

Pissed off and drunk at 3 a.m.
For the sake of getting into bed
All is to be assumed
About the health of that
Critter

## - MOTHER, FATHER -

Mother,
Why did I ever leave you
For I was not ready
To face the world
Or myself, nor be alone
I never really grew up
I am still a little boy
Afraid to make decisions
I wanted to come home
Smell your cooking

Father,
Why did you leave me
For I was not ready
You still had so much to show me
And I was so ready to learn from you
But as I grew tall,
Put away my toys forever
You were already gone

## - FLEET -

This fleeting moment
That is
Me

The blink of an eye,
That is
A lifetime
A nothing, compared to…

Let me grab a moment
Just this one perhaps
And let me hold it dear
As long as I like

Please,
Just this one

## - BIRDS -

The birds sing
But I don't hear them
The birds fly by my face
Weightless,
And dance before my eyes
But I don't see them
They are neither here nor there for me
They are nothing to me

I walk long and hard,
But never get anywhere
The same path for so many years
That brings me nowhere, anytime
Surrounded by so much life
I neither see nor hear
Smell nor taste
anything

# - LETTER FROM AN AMERICAN FARMER -

(in cultural exile in Germany)

Yo B.W.

What you be doin' man?
Hows the whether down in Florida?

Things be lookin' up, sometimes down
Gots me model trains runnin' finally
Like the big boys and
Big boobs you so loved

Made any snow penises lately?
Not easy down there
In the swamps
I can imagine

Getting' laid as much over there as you
Was here? Hope so!

My crops been greatly lately
Growin' up a storm, so to speak
Live like a king for once in my life
You knows what they say about
When your dreams come true,
So I been on the lookout, dude!

Well, stay in touch, I will let you know
When the record comes out

133

The street date,
As they say

Yours in perpetual and eternal friendship

Big Red

Ps.
When you comin' back?

## - TOKEN APPEARANCE -

My paintings cry
Aksala could change the world
If they'd only give it a chance
The sky is my only visitor
The sun gives me color, theory
The gift of its love

Across the street
From the gallery
The TV sets give off their
Blue glow, as far as the eye
Can see
Somewhere, hidden behind the curtains
And furniture, just out of sight
Lurks an entertainment
Junkie
Art-starved,
Manipulated zombie
Shitheads
At least one per TV

My gift for you is my soul, my truth
But you don't care
Because the tv commercials
Are not long enough
For a token appearance

## - FREEDOM FRIES -

Bush's monster
Bush's war
Bush's dinner's:
Freedom fries!

Saddam's oil
To power our grills
So we can munch:
Freedom fries!

Freedom kissing
Barbara's bush
We're all puking:
Freedom fries!

Pass the syrup
For freedom toast
At Bush's breakfast:
Freedom fries!

Iraqi lives
Iraqi blood
Iraqi ketchup for:
Freedom fries!

Freedom kissing
Freedom toast
We're all laughing cuz of:
Freedom fries

## - CANCER -

Christ,
I am so fucking afraid
Of getting cancer

That fear
Gnaws on me
Envelopes me, destroys
Inspiration, creation
Like an old bone
I am thrown to the dogs
For decay

White walls
Institution
Ill-behaved nurses
Needles, beeping machines
And pseudo cures
I am not sure if I am more afraid
Of the disease
Or the treatment

The ghosts
Of those gone or soon to be
Haunt me already
So young, inspiring
They will never again
Experience beauty
All that I blindly
Take for granted

## - GIVEN TO US -

The night
Is given to us
In order that we see heaven
Yearn for it
But reality is our gravity
It keeps us down
In a hell
That we built ourselves

The sun
Is given to us
To remind us every single day
That we are a prisoner
Of our own inventions
In a hell
That we built ourselves

The sun shines down on forests
Not of green,
But of gray concrete
The steel that separates us
And glass that reflects my tears

To look at the stars
Filled with an incredible longing
For an understanding of purpose
And for a knowledge that is still
Forbidden

I am struck down
By the realization
Of my worthlessness
Less,
Than a speck of sand on a beach
Than the blink of an eye
Than a thought

I think of our love,
And am filled with
An incredible longing
For an understanding
Of our purpose together
For a forbidden feeling
True love can only be forbidden

But then I am struck down
By the realization
Of my own worthlessness
For we are less than
What you claim we are
A grasp at an image
Too pure for this world,
Forbidden

## - NOBODY CARES -

Nobody cares
That the old lady in the old folk's home
Just died
Not even her husband
Even if his Alzheimer's would let him
Remember her
Because he was out fucking
Teenage tarts for years
Anyway

Nobody cares
That a little girl from the slums
Without family, without hope
Was raped and murdered
Last week
Not his killer
Nor the police
Nor her parents
Who sold her off as a baby
Anyway

Nobody cares
That Paul Klee is dead
But as his colors fade
The art history books
Will be burned
Anyway

Nobody cares
That John Lennon was murdered
Not any of his former
Screaming fans
From Shea Stadium
As they struggle with old age
Nor the shallow pop singers of today
Too preoccupied with their hair
And how they look on their
Youtube channels
Anyway

## - MACHINE -

They say a man's home
Is his castle
But I've built the walls so high
And put so many locks
On the door
That I can't get out anymore
And feel the sunshine
Of your humanity

For the first time ever
I feel I could throw it all away
Like the worthless trash it just might be
If I knew I could become
The garbage man of your dreams

So here I stand before you
Joe
Master of arrogance and
Verbal blunders

Naked and vulnerable
Without walls to protect me
Do you like
What you see?

Yes,
You intimidate me, scare me
For you show me what I have become
Cynical, inhuman

And what I am not:
A robot, of mechanized emotions
Mechanically creating

It would be so easy
To fall in love with you
Your beauty, intellect
And respect for humanity

## - WONDER WANDA -

I can't get no lovin'
I can't get no hole
My life is so grim,
Wonder Wanda

We can't find a drummer
We're losing our sound
Everything sucks,
Wonder Wanda

She writes all our words
She gives us our sound
She blows us backstage,
Wonder Wanda

She was a rock goddess
She took too many drugs
A punk rock legend,
Wonder Wanda

She couldn't take the pressure
She deflated on stage
She had to leave the band,
Wonder Wanda

(drum solo)

## - MY SUN IS ALWAYS SETTING -

Got that bad feeling
Don't go away no more
My sun is always setting
Dawn will never come

Attacked from all sides
Just a little boy
Don't think I'll ever learn
To cope with this world

My sun is always setting
Days are growing shorter
Days are growing colder
The day is about to die

The endless night is coming
The night it wants to kill me
The night it wants my blood
The night has killed my sun

My sun is always setting
My sun is always setting…

## - CYCLOPS IN THE SUN -

It's the little things
That I long for
With such force

The single lamp of the streetcar
So far away still, but coming
As the tracks appear to ripple
In the summertime heat
Of those endless summer days
Back when life was good,
Healthy and naïve
Back when my eyes were still good
And I was willing to listen

## - NOWHERE -

I have no land
To call my own
Neither a plot of land
To plan a future
Nor a country
That craves my soul
Neither here nor there
I live in
Nowhere

## - SCHITZO -

Schitzofrenia
Schitzolamia
Schitzogameia
Schitzosameia

Here, stop, try that
Nope, didn't work
That sounds right
Oops, nope. Stop, dead end!

Collection of false starts
And failed style attempts

To be everywhere at once
And yet
Always insufficient
Lost

## - EVENING RED -

I walk, sit, stroll
Only to think of you,
Gone

It is time to abandon
Dispatch enemy thoughts, and
Ultimately,
Petty feuds
And finger pointing

The smell of old wasted river water
Dying tadpoles, spotted
With disease
Reminds me of youth
And you,
Enjoying your young years

Energetic, gifted for words
How you dazzled these naïve ears
You spoke and we all listened
We all
Wanted to be your friend

Evening came, red with mission
You wanted so,
To touch the world
With your art
To be a part of "it"
Whatever that is

Evening stays
Red with hate
For the unfulfilled...

Damn you!
Why not just one more word
Or
A last goodbye
My
Dear
Friend

Herstellung und Verlag:
BoD - Books on Demand, Norderstedt
ISBN 978-3-7519-8319-8